Mike Harris'
TRAVEL GUIDES

OLVERA STREET™
Discover the Soul of Los Angeles

Mike Harris

La Frontera Publishing
Cheyenne, Wyoming

Olvera Street™
Discover the Soul of Los Angeles

Mike Harris' Travel Guides
Copyright © 2015 Michael T. Harris
All rights reserved.

Cover design, book design and typesetting by
Yvonne Vermillion and Magic Graphix

Printed and bound in the United States of America

First Edition
First Printing April 2015
ISBN: 978-0-9857551-8-8

Published by La Frontera Publishing
Cheyenne, Wyoming
(307) 778-4762 • www.lafronterapublishing.com

Dedication

To my mother, Agnes L. Raymond, who early on in my
life instilled in me a love for California's early history,
of its missions, rancheros and legendary characters,
and as a boy first took me to visit Olvera Street.

CITY HALL

PARKING LOT 1

Masonic Hall (1858)

Merced Theatre (1870)

Pico House (1869-70)

Vickrey Brunswig Building (1888)

La Plaza House (1883)

La Plaza de Cultura y Artes

Old Camp Santo (1826-4...

NORTH

SANCHEZ STREET

Chinese American Museum (Garnier Building, 1890)

Hellman Quon Building (1900)

Plaza Firehouse Museum (1884)

Founders Plaque

Kiosko

NORTH LOS ANGELES STREET

PARKING LOT 4

Old Plaza est. 1824

PASEO DE LA PLAZA

La Plaza Methodist Chur... (1925-26)

El Pueblo Offices (Biscailuz Buildin... 1925-26)

AED
Automatic External Defibrilator

$ ATM

Restrooms

Disabled Access

Information

101 FWY ENTRANCE

Old Chinatown Boundary

Fr. Serra Park (est. 1970)

Placita de Dolores (est. 1979)

101 FWY ENTRANCE

PARKING LOT 5

Path of the zanja madre (Mother Ditc...

LITTLE TOKYO

NORTH ALAMEDA STREET

UNION STATION

Map courtesy of El Pueblo de Los Angeles Historical Monument

El Pueblo de Los Angeles

HISTORICAL MONUMENT DIRECTORY

The Birthplace of Los Angeles

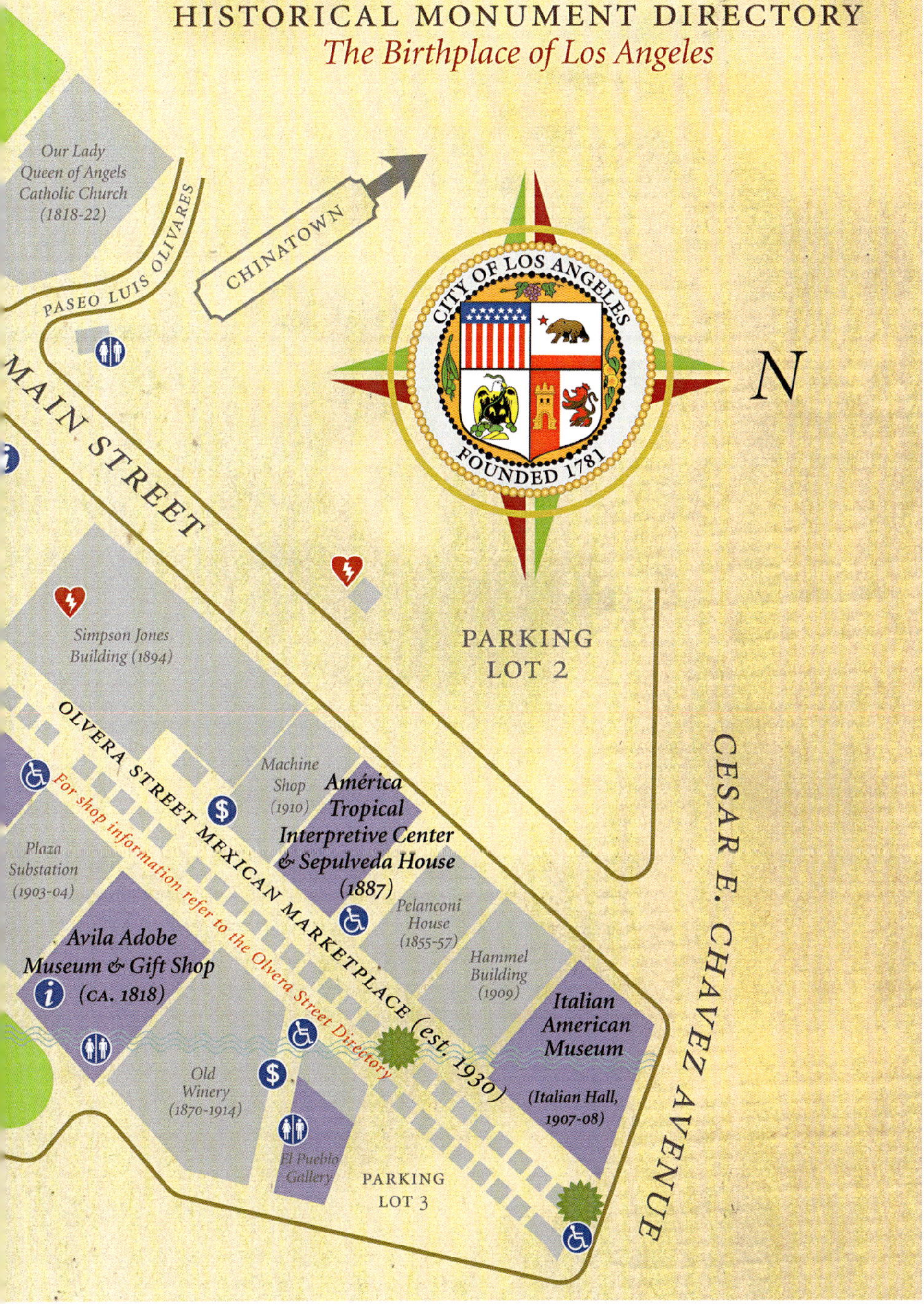

Our Lady Queen of Angels Catholic Church (1818-22)

PASEO LUIS OLIVARES

CHINATOWN

CITY OF LOS ANGELES · FOUNDED 1781

N

MAIN STREET

Simpson Jones Building (1894)

PARKING LOT 2

OLVERA STREET MEXICAN MARKETPLACE (est. 1930)

For shop information refer to the Olvera Street Directory

Machine Shop (1910)

América Tropical Interpretive Center & Sepulveda House (1887)

Plaza Substation (1903-04)

Avila Adobe Museum & Gift Shop (CA. 1818)

Pelanconi House (1855-57)

Hammel Building (1909)

Italian American Museum

(Italian Hall, 1907-08)

Old Winery (1870-1914)

El Pueblo Gallery

PARKING LOT 3

CESAR E. CHAVEZ AVENUE

Preface

One of my earliest memories as a boy growing up in Los Angeles in the early 1950s is taking my grandmother Edna's hand on a warm summer's morning, leaving my mother's house and walking through the front gate. Then the two of us would stroll a couple of blocks so we could catch a yellow and green-colored streetcar that would take us downtown.

Mind you, these are snapshot memories, because I could not have been more than four or five. But the flashes I see in my mind today are of climbing what was to me two or three gigantic steps into the streetcar, walking past the driver and sitting down on a bench seat next to grandma. Other memories of that day include watching cars and buildings whiz by, then the two of us stepping off the streetcar in downtown Los Angeles. I recall looking into shop windows and up at what were to me very tall stone buildings, all the time tightly holding grandma's hand.

My family's Los Angeles roots go back more than a century; not as long as some families, such as the descendants of the city's founders. Those original settlers (known as pobladores), forty-four in all with four soldiers along to guard them, included men, women and children. They walked from northwest Mexico to settle in the area that would eventually become El Pueblo de la Reina de Los Angeles (translation: the Town of Our Lady Queen of the Angels) on Sept. 4, 1781, the city's official founding date.

The descendants proudly call themselves Los Pobladores (the townspeople) after the original pobladores. Each year family members walk the roughly nine miles from the San Gabriel Mission to Los Angeles to mark the city's birthday.

With this travel guide, I celebrate that founding pueblo and the world-class city that evolved out of it.

Contents

Introduction

Forget L.A.'s glitzy bars and eateries, ignore the skyscrapers and high-rises, walk past those trendy stores. We're hunting for this great city's past, back more than 230 years ago when the pobladores walked from Mexico to start a new life in California. Today we're going to find those roots by visiting Olvera Street and El Pueblo de Los Angeles Historical Monument.

Many historic buildings important to the city's development were torn down long ago, and even some areas, such as the city's first Chinatown, were relocated. But there are landmarks of Los Angeles's history that remain, and thankfully they include some from the earliest days of El Pueblo de la Reina de Los Angeles, including the Avila Adobe, the La Placita Church, and several buildings from the mid to late 1800s.

Of course, the pobladores didn't come directly to the area around what is now downtown Los Angeles. They first stopped at Mission San Gabriel Arcángel, in what is now the City of San Gabriel, east of downtown Los Angeles. There, they rested, crying children and all. Later, the forty-four

El Pueblo's Plaza kiosko, with the Pico House in the background.

pobladores (making up eleven families) set off under an escort of soldiers and priests, crossed the Los Angeles River (then called *El Río de Nuestra Señora La Reina de Los Ángeles de Porciúncula*) and started a pueblo (Spanish for town).

Where it all began is now preserved.

They had a plan to follow, developed by Felipe de Neve, then governor of Spain's Californias. The story goes that de Neve was under orders from King Carlos III to start a pueblo, along with developing an economy, so to speak. Why the rush? Spain was getting nervous about British and Russian exploration taking place along the Pacific coast. Settling Upper California for Spain was becoming a priority, from San Diego to San Francisco.

De Neve took his assignment very seriously. By May of 1780 he had come up with a complete set of plans for the new pueblo (the location suggested by Father Juan Crespi) including where buildings should go, a church, farms and access to the river. Crespi had spotted the area during an exploration trip he and Father Junípero Serra took with explorer Gaspar de Portolà in 1769. The area along the river supported a population of native peoples known as the Tongva. Many of the Tongva later worked as laborers at the pueblo, in the ranches around the pueblo and at the San Gabriel Mission.

But I digress.

The original pueblo site, including a plaza, moved a couple of times due to flooding, and finally was washed away by a flood during the winter of 1814-1815. The Los Angeles River, long before it was confined in today's concrete and steel channel, was a flood plain, and in a heavy storm the water went where it wanted. A "new" pueblo and plaza were built to the northwest on higher ground, a safer location from flooding. That plaza also washed away three years later, according to the Los Angeles Department of Water and Power. In 1818 plans for a new plaza and Catholic chapel were developed. The third site is what we'll be exploring today.

The forty-plus acres inside the borders of El Pueblo de Los Angeles Historical Monument roughly represents the historical geographical center of Los Angeles. It is bounded by Spring Street, East Cesar Chavez Avenue, Alameda and Arcadia Streets (and the Hollywood Freeway).

The state, Los Angeles County and Los Angeles City officials all got together in 1953 to turn the area into a state park district, and in 1989 it was handed over to the City of Los Angeles to run.

El Pueblo includes twenty-seven historic buildings, and some wonderful artwork. There are many "firsts" located in and around the "Monument," as some local officials now casually refer to it. What's even more amazing for Los Angeles, several "firsts" are still standing. Here you'll find the first city-owned firehouse, the oldest still-standing fired brick building built in Los Angeles (Pelanconi House), the first three-story hotel (Pico House), the first building built expressly for theatrical purposes (Merced Theater), the oldest church in the city (La Placita), and the Avila adobe, built in 1818 and still standing as the oldest existing residence in the city.

Of course, there would be no Olvera Street, and certainly no

Statue of Father Serra in Father Serra Park.

historical monument, without the efforts (sometimes nagging, sometimes cajoling) by San Francisco Bay area socialite Christine Sterling, who led Los Angeles movers and shakers to preserve and renovate the area, and in 1930 to create a Mexican-style marketplace. More on her later on.

I really love visiting Olvera Street, and El Pueblo de Los Angeles Historical Monument, of which Olvera Street is the core. Whenever I go there, I usually find

La Plaza's statue of Governor Felipe de Neve.

something new to see, or learn something new about its history. And I love seeing the bright colors, smelling the aromas of Mexican food cooking, walking past the many vendor stalls in the middle of the street selling a variety of curios, and exploring the shops that offer Mexican clothing, furniture, tiles and artwork. Many years ago, I found in one of the shops a small, hand-made and hand-painted clay nativity scene, done in a modern, almost impressionistic style. It goes up on my family's fireplace mantle every Christmas.

With that in mind, I want to share with you my favorite things to see around Olvera Street. I hope you'll join me in visiting Olvera Street and El Pueblo using this personal travel guide, imagining those early times when the pueblo was founded, and exploring the city's rich heritage.

La Plaza

Location: Across from Father Serra Park.

Things to See: Plaza bandstand, Los Pobladores Founders' plaque, and statues of *Carlos III of Spain* and *Felipe de Neve* by Henry Lion.

Our first stop on our journey into the city's history is the Plaza. Established somewhere between 1824 and 1830 at the site we're visiting today, the Plaza has served as a community gathering area for residents and visitors ever since. But there have been a few changes. The Plaza used to be a rectangular shape, and had to be moved more than once because of flooding. The Plaza also was the location for the city's first above ground brick reservoir. Around 1871 the Plaza was trimmed down to a round design and landscaped, making it into a public park. In 1875 the city removed the reservoir and added a fountain. In 1962 a covered bandstand / kiosk with wrought-iron railing was erected and the fountain removed.

There are three main public entrances to the Plaza and El Pueblo. Some visitors approach the Plaza from the West, entering from North Main Street (there are two public parking lots, Lot 1 and Lot 2); some from the east, entering from Alameda Street and the Union Station transit center (there are three public parking lots, Lot 3 and Lot 5 on Alameda Street and the small Lot 4 on North Los Angeles Street); and some from the north, entering from Cesar E. Chavez Avenue, walking up Olvera Street and past the many eateries, shops and stalls.

The easiest approach for me personally is from the east, where I usually take Metro Rail or Metrolink trains into Union Station when I visit downtown Los Angeles.

By the way, Union Station is the largest railroad passenger terminal in the Western United States, and it is another of the city's historical jewels. But in the 1920s planning for a new rail terminal nearly wiped away the Plaza area. We'll get around to that part of our story a little later on.

If you're coming from the Union Station side, like I did today (yes, I always gaze up at the beautiful chandeliers hanging from the ceiling in

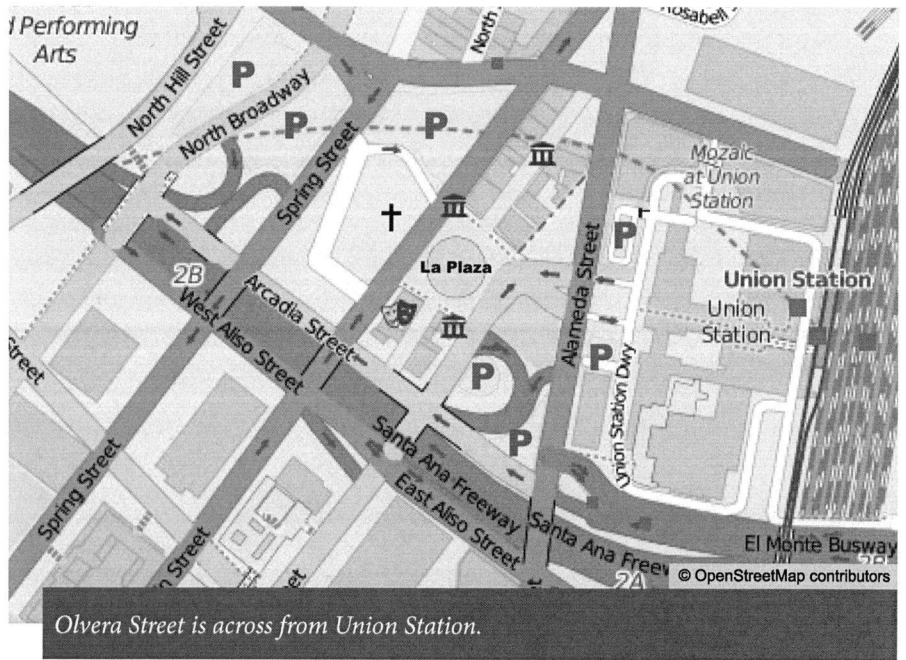

Olvera Street is across from Union Station.

The main entrance to El Pueblo from Union Station.

the lobby), you walk out of the primary entrance, past the old parking lot, and to the traffic signal on Alameda Street. Ahead is your first view of the entrance to the Plaza. Wait for the "pedestrian walk" signal at the traffic light, then head straight ahead.

Once across the street, on the right is the Placita de Dolores area, and as you walk along you'll see a very special bell. It is a replica of the Bell of Dolores, commemorating Mexican independence from Spain. Off to your left will be Father Serra Park, (just across North Los Angeles Street) named for Father Junípero Serra, with a large bronze statue of him. The

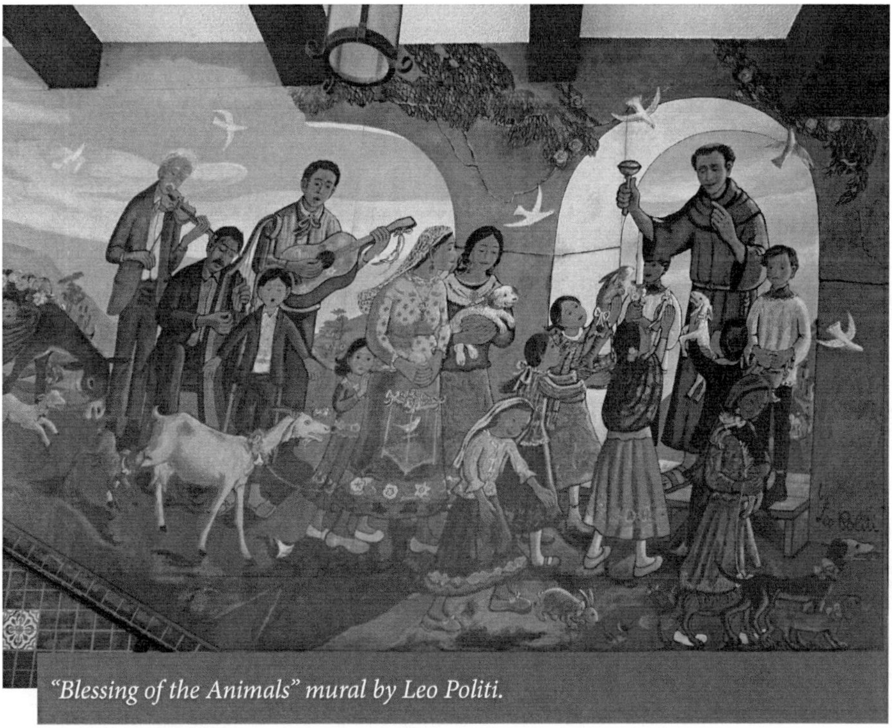

"Blessing of the Animals" mural by Leo Politi.

tiny park is unstaffed, unlocked and open from dawn to dusk.

We've almost reached the Plaza. Keep walking and to your right is the Biscailuz Building; take a moment to enjoy "The Blessing of the Animals" mural, painted in 1978 by noted artist Leo Politi. A little further is the entrance to the Plaza Methodist Church and its beautiful stained glass image of the Christ. But don't go in yet. That's later on our tour.

Off to the left, we can really see the Plaza now, with its brick planters and big trees. If we walk a little further, to the right is the entrance to Olvera Street. Instead of walking into Olvera Street, walk with me over to the Plaza, our first stop on this tour.

The Plaza is large and very inviting, with red brick low walls, seating areas, planters, and walkways. From a landscape point of view, the four massive Moreton Bay fig trees dominate, planted from seeds circa 1878. I enjoy the shade of those huge fig trees on L.A.'s hot summer days.

At the Plaza, expect to see lots of people relaxing and chatting, and visitors taking pictures.

Also located here are large bronze statues of the two men who were important to the town's settling: King Carlos III of Spain, and Governor de Neve. The governor's likeness is an artist's representation, since no images of de Neve are known to exist.

There are a number of bronze pavement plaques scattered around, commemorating historical events and the eleven original families who settled the pueblo, and they'll give you a bit more flavor of early L.A.'s founding.

At the Plaza, expect to see lots of people relaxing and chatting, and visitors taking pictures. Lunch time entertainment usually can be found seven days a week from around 11 a.m. to 4 p.m., with a variety of performers playing near the bandstand (also referred to as the kiosk, or kiosko, in Spanish), ranging from Aztec dancing and flute playing to salsa, meringue and mariachi music. On weekends you might find special events.

Many festivals also radiate from the Plaza. Some of the most colorful festivals at the historical monument include Blessing of the Animals, Cinco de Mayo, Mexican Independence Day, Fiesta de las Flores, Los Angeles City Birthday, Virgen de Guadalupe Day, El Dia de los Muertos (the Day of the Dead), and Las Posadas, a candlelight procession by children through Olvera Street depicting the journey of Mary and Joseph as they looked for a room in Bethlehem. There are other festivals and celebrations, and I'll detail those and the ones I've just mentioned later in this guide.

Sometimes I'll grab a quick lunch—maybe a soda and a couple of taquitos with guacamole sauce—sit on one of the Plaza's benches and just people watch.

You'll see groups of school kids out on field trips, visitors stepping off their big tour buses parked along North Main Street, or families strolling the Plaza. What languages will you hear? Everything from Spanish, German and Swedish, to French, Mandarin and plenty more. Olvera Street is a major international attraction.

Located around the Plaza are some of the city's historic gems.

Located around the Plaza are some of the city's historic gems. They include Pico House (1869-70), the Merced Theatre (1870), Masonic Hall (1858), the Hellman Quon Building (1900), the city's first firehouse (1884) and now the Plaza Firehouse Museum, the Garnier Building (1890) and now home of the Chinese American Museum, the Biscailuz Building (1925-26), the La Plaza United Methodist Church (1925-26), and the site of the Museum of Social Justice, and the Simpson Jones Building (1894).

Across Main Street is La Iglesia de Nuestra Señora la Reina de Los Angeles, or The Church of Our Lady the Queen of the Angels (1818-22) Catholic Church, also known simply as La Placita Church, the Campo Santo cemetery (1826-44), La Plaza House (1883) and the Vickrey Brunswig Building (1888). These last two are now the home to LA Plaza de Cultura y Artes, the area's center of Mexican American culture and history.

Some of the buildings aren't open to the public, some are used for events and displays, while others are museums. The Plaza United Methodist Church and La Placita Church continue to hold services, and in fact, La Placita Church has continuously been serving the downtown Los Angeles Catholic community since it was dedicated in 1822.

Before we leave the Plaza, I want to tell you about Las Angelitas del Pueblo, a non-profit organization of volunteers that offers free walking tours of El Pueblo de Los Angeles Historical Monument. The group's name translates as Little Angels of the City. You can find the group's office in the southeast corner of the Plaza, next to the Old Plaza Firehouse Museum. Las Angelitas docents take visitors on a fifty-minute tour around El Pueblo that covers many aspects of those early days when Los Angeles was just getting started. You'll find the group's web site at http://lasangelitas.org/ and tours are offered Tuesday through Saturday at 10 a.m., 11 a.m. and noon, as well as by reservation. A reservation is not necessary during their regular hours of service, but you might call or use their website beforehand if you want to plan ahead.

Now, let's get going to our second stop on our tour, the Plaza Firehouse Museum.

Plaque honors the original Los Pobladores families.

Plaza Firehouse Museum

Location: Old Plaza Firehouse, 1884.

Open: Tuesday through Sunday 10 a.m. to 3 p.m.

Admission: Donation requested.

Things to See: Restored 1880s horse-drawn fire engine, rotating fire engine turntable, historic photos, and a collection of firefighter helmets.

Just a few steps away from the Plaza is the Old Plaza Firehouse, the oldest firehouse in the City of Los Angeles. Built in 1884, it was "The first building to be constructed by the City of Los Angeles for housing firefighting equipment and personnel," according to the Los Angeles Fire Department's archives.

The Plaza Firehouse is now a museum, and it gives us a peek into what fighting fires was like in the late 1800s. Since fire engines back then were pulled by horses, the Plaza Firehouse offered some state-of-the-art

Above: Engine No. 1, the centerpiece of the museum.

equestrian features. First, the horses were stabled inside the station. The architect, William Boring, was from Illinois where keeping horses inside was the custom in colder climates. He liked the idea, so he incorporated that feature in his design. Second, a unique turntable in the floor made it unnecessary to back the horses in or out. It's another distinctive feature of the old building. Whether the turntable was ever used is uncertain. You'll also see the restored brass fireman's pole (no, we can't try it out), horse stalls and a hayloft.

Construction began in May 1884 on the brick building and work was completed by mid-August. The station housed the volunteer company known as the Original 38's. The volunteers moved in on Sept. 16, 1884, with Engine Company No.1. But the city found volunteer firefighters somewhat challenging to manage, so in December 1885 the city established its first paid fire department. The old

No, you can't slide down the old fire pole.

"volunteer 38's" were moved to the eastside of the city and then faded into history. By the way, they were called Original 38's because their roster numbered just thirty-eight men.

The Plaza Firehouse operated as a fire station until 1897, when it fell into a variety of ever-more-seedy uses. Those included a saloon, cigar store, pool room, flop house, warehouse and even a drugstore. Finally, in the 1950s the building was restored and in 1960 it became a firefighting museum.

The Firehouse was refurbished by the California State Division of Architecture, and remodeling followed as accurately as possible: "The original known conditions [were] based upon old photographs,

The old cupola bell tower also has been restored, but there's no bell. It's been missing since the turn of the nineteenth century...

records, publications, and 'reading the walls' of the structure as the work progressed. Much of the material used for restoration came from other old buildings of the approximate same period," according to an historical American buildings survey completed by the National Park Service in September 1963.

Curiously, during the restoration work, crews found a variety of items, such as the original iron door hinges bolted to the wall and an abundance of Chinese lottery tickets scattered all over the lower floor. The old cupola bell tower also has been restored, but there's no bell. It's been missing since the turn of the nineteenth century when the cupola was damaged, some say either by fire or blown down by the wind.

Inside the museum you'll find lots of historic photos, a collection of firefighter helmets, clocks, bells, a hand-drawn fire apparatus and old "Number 1," a restored horse-drawn fire engine from the 1880s. I want to give a special "pat on the back" to the members of the Box 15 Club of Los Angeles, a group of fire buffs who volunteer their time on many fire department projects. Members have helped with the restoration of the Plaza Firehouse and

A restored fire engine from the early 1800s.

have donated historical artifacts for display. The group also supports the museum's staff.

I love visiting here, partly because as a kid growing up in Los Angeles I always thought it would be cool to be an L.A. firefighter. And when I think of how little these early firefighters had to work with, I wonder how Los Angeles ever made it into the twentieth century.

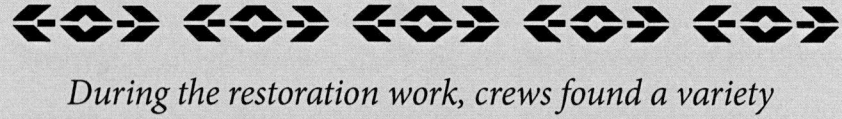

During the restoration work, crews found a variety of items, such as the original iron door hinges bolted to the wall...

Chinese American Museum

Location: Garnier Building, 1890.

Open: Tuesday through Sunday 10 a.m. to 3 p.m.

Admission: Donation requested.

Things to See: Sun Wing Wo General Store and Herb Shop, exhibits on Chinese immigration to the United States.

I want to take you next to the Chinese American Museum, the last surviving building of the city's original Chinatown, and Southern California's first museum solely dedicated to the Chinese American history and experience in and around Los Angeles.

But before we go inside, I want to show you a bronze plaque embedded in the sidewalk along North Los Angeles Street. It's on the eastern side of the historic Garnier Building, and if you reach Arcadia Street you've gone too far. If you're not looking for it, odds are you'll step right over it, but you shouldn't. Stop, look down and read what it says about a very

Above: The entrance to the Chinese American Museum.

dark, bloody and savage time in the City of Los Angeles's history.

The headline on the plaque is simple, yet terrifying. It reads: "Chinese Massacre." It should read, "Night of Shame, Terror and Horror."

The plaque marks that night on October

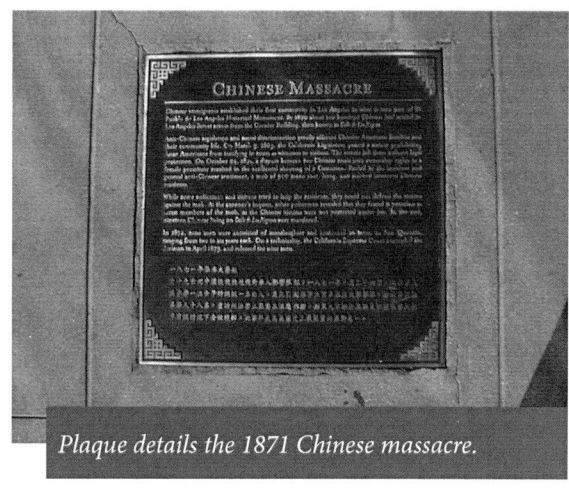

Plaque details the 1871 Chinese massacre.

24, 1871, when a racially motivated mob of around 500 mostly white men rioted and brutally beat, tortured and finally murdered nineteen Chinese men and boys by lynching them. The rioters also sacked many Chinese stores in what was then a growing Chinatown, stealing just about anything they could get their hands on. Almost every Chinese person the mob could find in the area around Calle de los Negroes (Street of the Negroes) was beaten and robbed.

The violence that night reflected the city's frontier history during the second half of the 1800s when lawlessness was tolerated, even sometimes condoned, as vigilantism was not uncommon. From what I've read about those days, lynching nineteen Chinese males was not outside of the city's culture.

While Los Angeles was founded by Spanish settlers (there were several of Indian, African or mixed race descent among the forty-four pobladores), it later developed from the influx of others, including Chinese, Italian and French.

You can experience the Chinese role in helping to forge what is today's Los Angeles by visiting the Chinese American Museum at El Pueblo de Los Angeles Historical Monument.

The address officially is 425 N. Los Angeles Street, but the entrance is on Sanchez Street, a leftover one-block-long street from those frontier days of the late 1800s. Look for a red brick building with shaded lights

View from the museum's second floor.

above the entrance and the words, "Chinese American Museum" above a green front door.

Let's go inside.

The building itself, the Garnier Building, was built in 1890 by French settler and businessman Philippe Garnier. The reason why it is the oldest surviving Chinatown building is because in the early 1930s much of old Chinatown was torn down to construct Union Station, just across Alameda Street. The rest of old Chinatown was slowly demolished, with the last remaining buildings gone by 1950 to make room for part of the Hollywood Freeway and Civic Center projects. The Garnier Building also is the oldest and most significant Chinese building in any of California's major metropolitan areas. Why? The original San Francisco Chinatown buildings were destroyed by the 1906 earthquake.

The Chinese American Museum takes up three floors of the Garnier Building. Step inside and you'll start to see some of the Chinese community's art and history.

A *display catches a visitor's attention.*

One of my favorite exhibits inside the museum is the Sun Wing Wo General Store and Herb Shop. It is a recreation of an actual store that opened in 1891 in the Garnier Building and operated there until 1948. I enjoy looking at the various types of merchandise that would have been sold at the Sun Wing Ho store, ranging from food and clothing to furniture and even firecrackers. The museum also recreated the herb shop where Chinese medicines were served up. And for the kids, there's even a wooden Chinese abacus to play with.

Upstairs you'll also discover exhibits on how the Chinese community grew in and around Los Angeles. One exhibit I really enjoyed recently was a variety of paintings and drawings done by Chinese-American students, giving me a view of how today's youth see Los Angeles and their communities.

The museum also recreated the herb shop where Chinese medicines were sold.

The general store's old cash register.

Museum of Social Justice / La Plaza United Methodist Church

Location: La Plaza United Methodist Church (1926).

Open: Thursday - Saturday from 10 a.m. to 3 p.m., Sunday 10 a.m. to 1 p.m., or by appointment.

Admission: Free. Donations requested.

Things to See: Historical documents, photographs and artifacts on the history of social change in Los Angeles; and a large stained-glass window of Jesus Christ.

Let's walk back across the Plaza, heading toward the entrance to the south end of Olvera Street, to visit the Museum of Social Justice, which is located in the La Plaza United Methodist Church. As we step from the Plaza, what greets us is the La Plaza United Methodist Church building, and next to it the Biscailuz Building. Both structures were built at the same time, between 1925-26. The Biscailuz Building is

Above: Entrance to La Plaza United Methodist Church and the Social Justice Museum.

now home to the Mexican Cultural Institute and the El Pueblo de Los Angeles Historical Monument's offices.

I love looking at the three-story church building, designed by Pasadena architects Train and Williams in Churrigueresque-style (Spanish Baroque and Rococo) characterized by elaborate surface decoration. My eyes first focus on the elaborate sculptural ornamentation framing the large wooden double doors and the stained-glass window featuring a welcoming Jesus Christ, with his arms and hands outstretched. Just below him are the words, *Venid a mi,* Spanish for "come to me."

To the left of the entrance is the tower. My eyes rise up along the wall to the top, where I see more sculptural ornamentation and a Moorish-style dome finished in green and yellow mosaic. The base of the dome is decorated with garlands, finials and panels, and the spire rises from the top.

Just below the dome is a round surface area, which puzzles me. It looks as if something should go there. Last year someone told me a clock face used to go there, but it has been "misplaced" and no one seems to

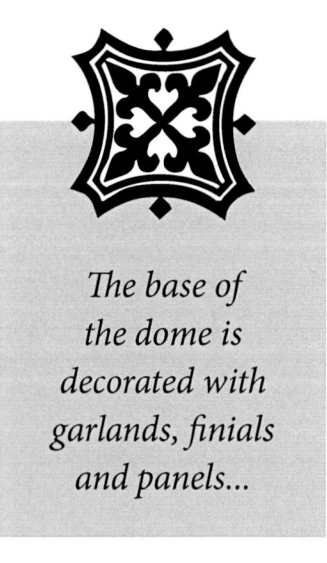

The base of the dome is decorated with garlands, finials and panels...

A Moorish-style dome tops the church's tower.

The church's stained-glass window features a welcoming Jesus Christ.

know what happened to it, sort of like the missing bell, which used to be in the bell tower that topped the Plaza Firehouse. When the firehouse was restored in the 1950s, no one involved could find any clue about what happened to the bell. Apparently, that's also the case for the church's missing clock face, if ever there was one.

To really see the beauty of the stained-glass window, just step up to the double doors. There you'll see a large mirror reflecting the beauty of the window and the Christ. If you step just inside and turn around, look up for the full impact. The first time I saw it during a summer day with the sun shining through a cloudless Los Angeles sky, it briefly took my breath away.

If you have time, walk inside the sanctuary of the church, where Sunday service is still held for the Plaza United Methodist Church members and visitors. The interior of the church and the sanctuary was altered in the 1960s, and when the work was done the altar was elevated. Because of the changes, I'm told that some of the feeling of the original church was lost.

Side entrance to the Museum of Social Justice.

I was never in the church before the remodeling, but I can say that whenever I walk inside I experience both a feeling of welcome as well as a warmth that seems to say to me "be at peace."

The Museum of Social Justice is located in the basement, and to reach it I either take the interior stairs, or just outside at the base of the bell tower there are outside doors that lead down to the exhibits. Because there is so much to see, keep a good eye out for the signage next to the door. You might walk past it.

The museum's historical collection includes documents, more than 2,000 photographs and artifacts gathered by church officials and volunteers covering Los Angeles from the start of the twentieth century to today. All of the collection provides visitors with a look into the struggle of immigrants, many of them Mexicans, trying to make a life in and around the city—the poor living conditions, social injustices committed against many of them and the efforts by many to improve conditions. Needless to say, La Plaza Methodist Church made a real difference for many of them.

Usually, there are volunteers on hand to answer questions, but if you're lucky enough to meet Leonora Barron, the museum's executive director, take time to talk with her about the Museum of Social Justice. Leonora is passionate about the museum and the many stories of immigrants trying to live and make a home in Los Angeles.

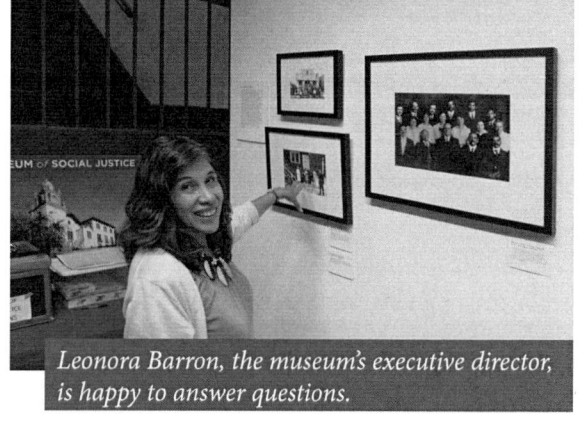

Leonora Barron, the museum's executive director, is happy to answer questions.

Puestos / Painted Booths

Location: All along Olvera Street.

Open: Daily, usually from 10 a.m. to 6 p.m.

Admission: Free.

Things to See: A range of merchandise and food, varying in prices.

The main entrance to Olvera Street is just a few steps away from the Plaza United Methodist Church and the Museum of Social Justice, and it's easy to spot. There's a large carved wooden cross to mark the entrance, and the cross's circular base, made up of three stone and mortar steps, makes it easy for visitors to pose for photos. The cross commemorates the September 4, 1781 founding of Los Angeles, and it was erected as part of the reconstruction of Olvera Street and the creation of a Mexican marketplace, which officially opened on Easter Sunday, April 20, 1930.

Olvera Street's Mexican marketplace attracts visitors from all over the world.

Olvera Street's wooden cross commemorates the city's 148th anniversary.

What you see today is not the original wooden cross commissioned in 1929 by Christine Sterling, the visionary for today's Olvera Street, for the city's 148th anniversary. The original cross, I'm told, is located across the street at La Placita Church. Today's wooden cross is the second cross to serve as the welcoming landmark. While it looks good, it is not in the best of shape, having weathered over time and suffering a bit from termites. I'm told a third generation wooden cross is in the planning.

The center of Olvera Street is made up of puestos (Spanish for booths) where merchants offer a variety of souvenirs, trinkets, jewelry, t-shirts, blankets, toys, sandals, candies, posters, shoes, gifts, and food and drinks. These small shops mostly run down the center of Olvera Street, and usually are no more than about 100 square feet in space. Some puestos line along the sides of the main buildings, but there are also larger retail stores and full-service restaurants that I'll write about later.

Sterling's idea was to create a Mexican marketplace somewhat resembling what you

A puesto merchant places merchandise for visitors.

Merchants offer a variety of souvenirs, trinkets, jewelry, t-shirts, blankets, toys, candies, and gifts.

would find in the cities and villages of Mexico, selling merchandise that also included handcrafted items. One of the things I like about this part of Olvera Street are the colors, the bright reds, yellows and greens everywhere. I also enjoy the smells of food being prepared, such as taquitos, tacos and red and green sauces.

Visitors enjoy outdoor shopping.

A stroll is the best way to enjoy the street. I suspect one of your first impressions will be how narrow is the passageway between the rows of puestos. The western side of the street has more room for walking. All of the shops are family-owned, some of them generational from when Olvera Street first opened in 1930. This outdoor shopping mall is a block long and tree-lined with welcoming shade during the summer. You'll even see grape vines hanging across the street near the center. And don't miss the old pepper tree near the Avila Adobe. Based on its size, I'm guessing it also dates from the 1930s.

Sometimes around noon, and especially on weekends, musicians wander the street, stopping every so often to play Mexican tunes for visitors. If you're sitting in one of the restaurants, expect to see a trio wander in to play music. If you ask for a tune, be sure to give them a tip. No change, please.

Strolling along Olvera Street, you'll also see a few points of interest, such as a sundial dedicated to Kit Carson, and a bluish-colored three-level fountain, also dating from 1930. Look down near the base and you'll see bricks laid out in a zig-zag pattern. That's to show the path of the Zanja Madre (pronounced zanha madre), Spanish for mother ditch. It used to bring water to the downtown area from the old Los Angeles River, and the first aqueduct to be built for the city. There's also a bronze plaque about the Zanja Madre.

Shade trees make summer outdoor shopping comfortable for visitors.

A sandstone trough dating from 1897 is one of Olvera Street's unique features.

At the northern entrance, there's a carved stone trough, donated courtesy of the city's Department of Water and Power. Some visitors might think it came from the 1800s around old Los Angeles. It wasn't. There's a plaque at the back of the trough that reads: "Sandstone trough used for feeding crushed acorns to livestock, hewn in 1897, by the Schweikand family on their San Fernando Valley ranch." Today, there are no crushed acorns, but there is water in the trough, much enjoyed by the birds who drop around for a quick drink.

While some might say that much of the merchandise sold at the puestos is very touristy, a friend of mine who frequently visits Olvera Street with his children offered a very interesting point of view.

"Where else could you go to a place where you can give your child a twenty dollar bill, let them go shop and then they go home with a lot of things that they'll have fun playing with for a while," he said. "Maybe a puppet, maybe a toy guitar, and a churro to eat. It's great!"

I have to agree.

Notes

_____

_____

_____

_____

_____

_____

_____

_____

_____

_____

_____

_____

_____

_____

_____

_____

_____

_____

_____

_____

_____

_____

America Tropical Interpretive Center

Location: Sepulveda House (1887).

Open: Tuesday - Sunday, 10 a.m. to 3 p.m.

Admission: Free; donations accepted.

Things to See: *America Tropical* mural by famed Mexican artist David Alfaro Siqueiros, and exhibits that historically explore the mural in its different contexts.

Wandering around Olvera Street, talking with the folks there, and seeing its many attractions always is fun for me. The street is so much more than that, though. Case in point is the America Tropical Interpretive Center, and the *America Tropical* mural painted in 1932 by noted Mexican revolutionary, artist and muralist, David Alfaro Siqueiros, and a group of students.

Not only is the *America Tropical* the last complete public Siqueiros mural left in Los Angeles (another mural was transported to the

Above: Inside the America Tropical Interpretive Center.

Santa Barbara Museum of Art), it also tells a story about cultural and political attitudes around Los Angeles at the time. The mural, measuring approximately 80 feet long by 18 feet high, was painted on the second story wall of the Italian Hall. As noted in a description about the mural on the Getty Conservation Institution's website, "*America Tropical* depicts a Mexican Indian, crucified on a double cross beneath an American eagle, with two sharpshooters taking aim at the eagle from a nearby rooftop."

Siqueiros was commissioned by local businessmen to paint the mural in 1932 and the image was supposed to depict a joyous, carefree Mexican scene of a tropical America. Siqueiros had other ideas, and the revolutionary in him came out. The image of the crucified peon was so politically charged and controversial that by 1938 it had been completely whitewashed, and for many years simply forgotten.

But there were those in the Los Angeles community who didn't forget, and in 1988 the Getty Conservation Institute and the City of Los Angeles agreed to conserve what was left of the faded mural and find a way for it to be viewed by the public.

Siqueiros's image of a crucified peon shocked many local businessmen.

Today's view of America Tropical's crucified peon is hard to see due to fading.

The nearly $10 million conservation effort included stabilizing the mural and constructing a protective canopy shelter, a public viewing platform and establishing an interpretive center to explain to the public what they would be seeing. Eighty years after its first unveiling, *America Tropical* reopened in 2012 for public viewing.

The mural and the interpretive center, located in the Sepulveda House, is a real historical jewel for El Pueblo. The entrance is roughly in the middle of Olvera Street on the west side. There are steps and a ramp that leads up to the entrance, and the interpretive center is on the left. Two rooms detail the history and political climate surrounding the mural. There is an elevator and stairwell that take you up to the second floor where you enter the viewing area. The mural is about fifty feet away and that's as close as you can get. It is somewhat hard to see after roughly eighty years of being covered up by paint, impacted by the hot summer sun and weathering. The Getty folks did a fantastic job of conserving what was there. There was no effort to restore the mural, partly because there are no color images of the mural and only the artist could repaint the mural to its original glory.

I get a much better view of the mural inside the interpretive center, which includes a complete scaled-down version and interpretive video screens for visitors to use to learn about various aspects of the mural.

I have to admit, during my many visits over the years to Olvera Street, up until the 1980s I had never even heard of Siqueiros and his controversial mural. Now, it is one of my favorite places to visit.

Look up to see a shrine to the Virgin Mary.

Also, as you head up the outside entrance, look up and you'll see a wooden Virgin Mary shrine. And just a bit further up the way before you enter the interpretive center is the Sepulveda House mini-museum.

A canopy shelter now protects the America Tropical mural.

Sepulveda Block Museum

Location: Sepulveda House (1887).

Open: Tuesday - Sunday, 10 a.m. to 3 p.m.

Admission: Free.

Things to See: A restored 1890s-era Eastlake Victorian-style kitchen and bedroom.

Since we've just visited the America Tropical Interpretive Center, and since we're "in the neighborhood," we might as well take a quick look at the Sepulveda Block Museum, giving us another view of the city's history.

I like looking at the displays because some of the items on view remind me of some of the household items I remember seeing my grandmother use around our house when I was a boy. You see, grandmother never threw away anything.

Above: Exterior view of the Sepulveda House.

Entrance to the Sepulveda Block Museum.

While we didn't have a wood-burning stove like the one on display, some of the kitchen utensils you'll see here are pretty close to what I saw in my youth. I remember she had a 1920s era hand-crank egg beater with a gawd-awful red-painted wooden handle and crank that I have and still occasionally use, especially for whipping up her wonderful recipe for egg nog. It's a lot of work, I'll tell you, but it brings back plenty of fond memories.

The Sepulveda House was built in 1887, and the building was

Señora Sepulveda's bedroom, as it might have looked.

The museum's entrance leads visitors to the kitchen exhibit.

designed in the Eastlake Victorian style. It had twenty-two rooms, with two commercial businesses on Main Street and three private dwelling rooms in back. It was built by Señora Eloisa Martinez de Sepulveda, who had great hopes for the area around the pueblo, hopes that never materialized during her later years.

The kitchen exhibit shows what Señora Sepulveda's meal preparation would have looked like, right down to the beautiful stove, skillets and pans. The bedroom exhibit shows how Señora Sepulveda's room would have looked, including a canopied bed, wood-burning stove and marble top dresser with swivel mirror.

There's also a display panel just inside the entrance detailing the history of the Sepulveda family and the property.

The front of the brick building on Main Street is impressive, with two large bay windows on the second floor, topped with an iron railing, and a triangle gable in the center. We'll see it later when we cross Main Street to visit some of the other stops on this tour.

Notes

Avila Adobe House Museum

Location: Avila Adobe (1818).

Open: Daily, 9 a.m. to 4 p.m.

Admission: Free.

Things to See: A collection of 1840s-era furnished rooms, and an outside courtyard and garden offering an example of life in the rancho period of California.

I can't believe we almost lost the Avila Adobe to the bulldozer and the wrecking ball. But then, I can't believe that over the years we've lost so many of the city's architectural treasures, such as the beautiful black-and-gold Richfield Oil Tower at 555 South Flower Street, which was torn down in 1969 to make way for the Arco Plaza twin tower skyscraper complex (it's now called City National Plaza).

Built in 1818 by Francisco José Avila, a successful ranchero, the home has survived earthquakes (damage from the 1971 Sylmar temblor closed it until 1977), storms, an invasion by American military forces under

Above: Built in 1818, the Avila Adobe is the city's oldest existing house.

command of Navy Commodore Robert Stockton, economic depressions, crime and urban decay around downtown L.A.

It was the plight of the old, run down adobe house and its condemnation order from the city's Department of Health that on November 29, 1928 spurred Christine Sterling to take action to preserve it and eventually many of the properties around Olvera Street (which was a dirt alley at the time).

Leaving the America Tropical Interpretive Center, where we just visited, we'll walk across Olvera Street, past puestos to where the Avila Adobe is waiting for us. It is the center of the El Pueblo monument, and a major magnet for visitors, including groups of school children on field trips to learn about early Los Angeles's history.

Just outside the front of the building, next to wooden steps on one side and a bench on the other, is a sign telling visitors they have reached the Avila Adobe, with a bit of information about its early history. The entrance to the museum is along the southern side of the building, and there is a sign attached to a wall that reads "The Avila Adobe" and "Entrance"

A child's cradle, such as this one, would have been used by the Avila family.

An exterior sign offers details of the Avila Adobe.

and an arrow directing us to where we start the self-guided tour. Docents are available, if visitors have questions.

The outside of the front of the building, along with the full-length porch, is plain and really doesn't draw visitor attraction. But inside, that's where history comes alive in the adobe's rooms and the furnishings.

The first room we see, and the largest in the house, is the family room. At the center is a massive wood dining table, surrounded by benches and chairs. It is the type of table which the Avila family and guests would have used for formal meals. The table you see is a reproduction. Something like this would have been used for entertaining by Encarnacion (Sepulveda)

Señor Avila would have kept track of his ranch business at a desk similar to this one.

A massive wood dining table is on display.

Avila, Don Francisco Avila's second wife. His first wife died in 1822. Avila had three children from his first marriage, and three more from his marriage with Encarnacion, who was fifteen when she married him. He was fifty. Encarnacion was the daughter of Francisco Sepulveda, a friend of Avila's.

Above the table hangs a wrought iron chandelier, while more candles hang from the walls. Look at the windows, and note how thick the adobe walls are. Not only did the thickness help give them strength, it also kept rooms cooler in the summer and warmer in the winter.

Other rooms to view include the family room,

What the Avila bedroom might have looked in the 1840s.

Table and chairs from the 1840s period.

the parlor, the kitchen, bedrooms, and Don Francisco's office, where he would have attended to his businesses, including a vineyard and his ranch, the nearby Rancho Las Cienegas, about seven miles north of the pueblo. Avila and his family would have spent most of their time at the ranch, keeping the adobe for visits to the pueblo to do business, attend church and meet and dine with friends.

The kitchen would have been used for cooking meals when the weather was bad, while during good weather and in the summer, meals would have been made outside in the outdoor patio. The kitchen served another purpose as well. A large wooden tub in the middle of the room

Most of the summer cooking would have been done outside.

A replica of a carreta, a two-wheeled wooden cart, is displayed in the garden.

would have been used for family bathing. Each of the rooms are furnished with items from the 1840s period.

The tour leads us outside, where we can see the courtyard patio area and its large wood-fired oven, garden and towards the back and roped off, a carreta (a two-wheeled wooden cart or wagon pulled by mules or oxen that would have been used by pueblo settlers as the 1800s version of today's pickup truck).

The adobe was used briefly by Commodore Stockton following the invasion of California in 1846 by American forces, part of the Mexican-American War.

There is so much more to the history of the Avila Adobe, more than I can go into in this guide. For example, Sterling even lived in the Avila Adobe, once it had been restored, and gave tours to visitors until her death in 1963. The rich history of the adobe, and of El Pueblo, are some of the reasons I keep returning.

Each of the rooms are furnished with items from the 1840s period.

La Placita Catholic Church

Location: La Iglesia de Nuestra Señora la Reina de Los Angeles (1822); 535 North Main Street.

Open: Daily.

Admission: Free.

Things to See: The oldest church in Los Angeles.

Now I want to take you to a remarkable piece of El Pueblo's history, reaching back to the settlement's very early days, back to 1814 when La Iglesia de Nuestra Señora la Reina de Los Angeles, or in English, The Church of Our Lady the Queen of the Angels, began.

We're going to walk to the northern entrance to Olvera Street, past the sandstone trough, turning left at Cesar E. Chavez Avenue (and past the entrance to Las Anitas Restaurant). Then, we'll cross over Main Street and head south, past Parking Lot 2. As we walk, you can see to your left the exteriors of the Italian Hall (where supporters hope to open an

Above: The entrance to La Plaza Catholic Church, as seen from across Main Street.

La Placita's historical altar is beautiful and spiritually moving.

Italian-American Museum soon), and the Sepulveda House with its two large bay windows on the second floor.

Known by locals simply as La Placita Church, its roots actually go back to 1784 when priests from Mission San Gabriel established an *asistencia* mission on the banks of the Porciúncula River that flowed near the new settlement. That first mission outpost was later abandoned as growing numbers of settlers needed something more. Foundation stones were laid in 1814 for a new church, but the river overflowed (it did that a lot back then) and it was decided to relocate the foundation stones to their current location on higher ground. Even though it was completed in 1822, the Archdiocese of Los Angeles regards 1814 as the founding date.

We'll first come upon the courtyard at Mission Nuestra Senora Reina de Los Angeles, and you'll notice written above the archway that the church was founded on Sept. 4, 1781. This is a very busy church. On Sundays it offers eleven masses, and the baptisms are so popular that often you can see lines of waiting parents, godparents and friends. The courtyard is there for a variety of uses, including events for the holidays. Services

On the exterior is a beautiful mural, depicting the Annunciation.

are held in Spanish, since the parish is primarily made up of Spanish-speaking members, as it has been historically.

The entrance to the chapel is a little ways inside the courtyard, and on the left. Visitors are welcome, so walk in, and since it is an active church, even during weekdays you'll probably find people inside, sitting in the pews, thinking and praying. If you have time, take a seat and look around you. The altar area is beautiful and spiritually moving, and the ceiling is wonderful. The last time I visited the chapel, I finally noticed in the back a full-sized statue of Christ, lying on his back and with his eyes closed, and covered by a Plexiglas top. It looks quite old, and I'll bet there's an interesting story behind it.

You're in the chapel, the old, original part of the church. A much larger church was built in 1965 right in back of La Placita, with the main entrance off of Spring Street. When you're ready to move on, as you head back southward on Main Street, look up at the exterior of the church's entrance. High above on the old facade is a mosaic mural, a replica of the one on a Franciscan chapel near Assisi, Italy. It depicts the Annunciation of the Virgin Mary by the angel Gabriel. The mosaic was added to La Placita Church on its bicentennial.

The patio next to the chapel hosts many of La Placita's events.

Notes

La Placita Church Cemetery

Location: Next to the Plaza Catholic Church (1822).

Open: Viewing only from outside the memorial fence.

Things to See: Campo Santo Memorial Garden, and informative display signs.

F unny thing about history; sometimes it jumps up when you least expect it. Such is the case of the historic La Iglesia de Nuestra Senora de Los Angeles Cemetery.

As we leave La Placita Church, walking south on Main Street, just past the church is the fenced-in Campo Santo Memorial Garden, landscaped with native plants. The fence is decorative, and the pattern reminds me of growing trees, with their roots extending into the earth. A descriptive band that runs along each fence section includes a variety of words, such as "paz," "pobledores," "remember" and "ancestors."

Above: The Campo Santo Memorial Garden next to La Placita Church.

Display signs give visitors some of the early cemetery's history.

Site construction crews in 2010 uncovered bones from some of the early settlers.

A view of the restored cemetery as seen from across Main Street.

The words are written in five different languages, in addition to three Native American languages.

The cemetery was closed in 1844, and the remains of those buried there were exhumed and supposedly re-interred at the new Calvary Cemetery in the city. The church cemetery after that sort of faded into history. At the start of the twentieth century, commercial buildings were even erected on the property. According to reports, in 1950 Los Angeles County bought the block south of the church, including the Vickrey Brunswig Building (built in 1888) and the Plaza House, built in 1883. Three small commercial buildings, including one that was directly on top of the old cemetery, were torn down. The land was leveled, asphalted, and turned into a parking lot.

In 2001, the parking lot was removed and the area landscaped and fenced. Then in 2010 construction began on the site, part of the plans for the new LA Plaza de Cultura y Artes, a Los Angeles County Mexican

A walkway separates the garden from the back of the church.

museum and center for Mexican American culture. That's the next stop on our tour, by the way.

When crews started digging in the area of the old cemetery sometime in October, they began finding bones and other artifacts. But digging didn't stop until a loud enough public outcry forced the digging to halt in January 2011. After months of meetings with tribal representatives, community groups and descendants of the original pobladores, as well as with the National Park Service, the remains were re-interred in April 2012. The permanent fencing you see here, as well as the landscaping, make up the Campo Santo Memorial Garden (campo santo translates as consecrated ground) and includes the remains of descendants of Los Pobladores, Native Americans and other settlers.

When crews started digging in the area of the old cemetery sometime in October, they began finding bones...

LA Plaza de Cultura y Artes

Location: 501 North Main Street / Plaza House (1883) and Vickrey Brunswig Building (1888).

Open: Noon to 7 p.m., Monday through Sunday. Closed Tuesdays, and certain holidays.

Admission: Free; donation suggested.

Things to See: Calle Principal, a recreation of 1920s-era Main Street featuring a variety of stores reflecting the city's growing Mexican community, as well as galleries focusing on the history of Los Angeles.

The entrance to LA Plaza de Cultura y Artes is across from the Campo Santo Memorial Garden, and you can't miss the large purple banner that reads "Welcome." The interior layout is modern and inviting, and the galleries are well lighted with plenty of information about what you're seeing.

Above: The Calle Principal exhibit, inside LA Plaza de Cultura y Artes.

Exterior of LA Plaza de Cultura y Artes, right, with the federal courthouse and City Hall in the background.

The main attraction is Calle Principal, located on the second floor. Calle Principal is a recreation of Los Angeles's 1920s-era Main Street, and its growing Mexican-American community. At Calle Principal, you walk down a street with storefronts on either side. The stores include a portrait studio, a pharmacy, a neighborhood grocery store, a clothing store and a phonograph and record store. Walking the street and looking in the windows, you can get a bit of a feel for what daily life might have been back in 1920s Los Angeles.

Opened in April 2011, the center is still in its early stage of development, and an announced plan for a $235 million mixed-use development on two large nearby county-owned parking lots will

A display of women's clothing from the early 1800s.

Exhibits offer views of Mexican-American history from the early 1800s.

benefit the center's nonprofit La Plaza de Cultura y Artes Foundation. The project is still years away, but the foundation should see a boost in its annual revenues in the near future.

Because it's new, and with a tight budget, LA Plaza notes that it is not a collections museum, but receives historical items on loan from other museums and collections. As items are returned to their home collection, LA Plaza curators bring in new, relevant items.

You can't miss the entrance, just look for the big welcome banner.

LA Plaza also has its own cultural store, called La Tienda, where visitors can shop for jewelry from local and international artisans, books on Mexican history and culture, CDs and DVDs, home decor items and limited edition artwork.

Notes

Food and Shops

Location: All along Olvera Street.

Open: Daily, with extended hours during special events and summer weekends.

Two of the things I enjoy most about Olvera Street are the shops and the restaurants. I'm not talking about those puestos that cater mostly to tourists looking for a quick, inexpensive souvenir to take home for friends or coworkers, nor the quick walk-up counter food stands, although they're pretty good, and great if you're in a real hurry to catch a bus or train.

The stores I'm talking about offer specialty items, hand-crafted items that reflect art and culture. The restaurants I'm wild about are full-service, sit down affairs that leave you asking for more, even though you're stuffed. So I want to mention a few of my favorites to you, knowing you'll also find your own favorites the more you visit Olvera Street.

Above: Olvera Street offers quality handcrafted items, and great Mexican food.

Armando Murillo, busy at his leather shop's workbench.

First the shops.

Murillo Leather Goods is a second-generation leather craft store, now run by Armando and Lupita Murillo. Often you'll find Armando at his workbench just to the left as you enter his store. You'll find him stripping lengths of leather for belts, or tooling leather for a handmade ladies bag, or a man's wallet.

His parents, Manuel and Camerina Murillo, established the business in 1971, and Armando can remember as a boy watching his father create leather goods, occasionally helping and learning the business.

"We manufacture our own products, and we offer high quality leather work," he told me on one of my visits. Handcrafted items are hung everywhere in the store, from shoes and bags to vests and belts. "We have customers still coming to us for many years, because they know they'll find quality here," he says with a welcoming smile.

Another family-operated store I enjoy visiting is **Casa California**, run by Norma Garcia and her daughter, Valerie Hanley. The entrance is impressive, with two massive wooden doors that open wide, displaying a range of items, from jewelry and colorful piñatas to imported woodwork from Oaxaca and a large variety of religious items

Norma Garcia, right, and her daughter, Valerie Hanley, inside their Casa California store.

Martha Medina greets guests to her Olverita's Village store.

and imported statues.

"People enjoy our traditions and culture," Valerie told me. "We get lots of tourists visiting us, from places like Japan and Europe. And regular customers who keep coming back."

Just a little further along Olvera Street is **Olverita's Village**, owned and run by Martha Medina. Her store specializes in Mexican hand embroidered clothing from all regions of Mexico, including costumes for folklorico dance troops and Mariachi suits for men and women. Some clothing she can have handmade for you by a variety of tailors in Mexico. The stitching on the shirts I saw was excellent.

"I like to think that we are a window into the culture of Mexico," she explained.

She learned the business from her father, who owned a folk art distribution warehouse in the city of Tijuana, Mexico. He was one of the first Mexican art distributors to Southern California. "For 50 years, My father brought merchandise to Olvera Street," she said. She would come along sometimes.

She purchased Olverita's Village about twenty-five years ago, with the idea that she would follow her father's legacy of promoting Mexican folk art. Pieces she has in her store are unique and reflect popular art, such as paper mache pieces from the internationally renowned Linares family.

An unusual shop not far from the main entrance to Olvera Street is **Kitty's Sno-Cone**, run by Kitty Lynn. She inherited the business from her stepfather, who started it around 1977.

"He started with a popcorn wagon, and then started this," she said. Her sno-cones are popular. "Some days it's a twelve-hour day for me,"

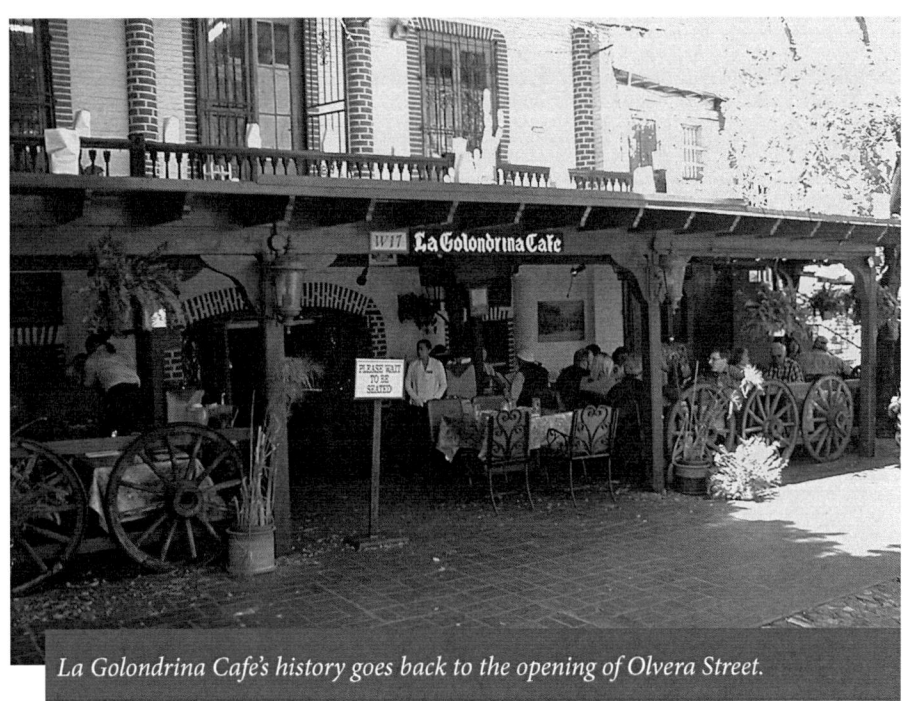

La Golondrina Cafe's history goes back to the opening of Olvera Street.

she said. But she meets some interesting people. "No matter what's happening in the city, it's happening downtown," she added. The favorite flavor? "It has to be the cherry sno-cone," she said, smiling.

Olvera Street offers some really great Mexican food, and you can either get it standing up at a walk-up counter, or visit one of the full service restaurants, including **La Luz del Dia** at the Plaza entrance, **Las Anita's Cafe** at the corner of Cesar Chavez Avenue, or at **La Golondrina Cafe** or at **El Paseo Inn**. These last two restaurants are almost directly across from each other in the middle of Olvera Street.

An inviting taco, enchilada and chile relleno combo plate from Las Anitas.

El Paseo's chile verde, served with rice, beans and handmade tortillas.

I enjoy cuisine at all of them, and each has its own little differences. For example, at **La Golondrina Cafe** there is a stone fireplace, and sometimes in the winter they'll have a fire. Sitting at a table in front of the fireplace with a friend while having a margarita is pretty nice. The food's excellent as well. At **El Paseo Inn**, you can watch someone make hand-made tortillas, which come to you hot off the griddle and thick, not like the thin tortillas you buy in packages at the supermarket. And good food.

Las Anitas Mexican Restaurant has been serving Mexican cuisine in the basement of the historic Italian Hall since 1947. It was started by Ana Natalia Guerrero, a founding Olvera Street merchant. Since you step

The exterior of El Paseo Inn and its outdoor patio.

down into the restaurant, the place feels cozy. The bar is just on the left as you enter. Everything is very colorful, from the bright wooden chairs to the paint on the walls. The menu is extensive, and the food is good.

La Luz del Dia is a cafeteria-style restaurant serving Michoacan Mexican food. The restaurant also makes its own tortillas, and you can watch them being made and grilled. You order at the counter, and there's plenty of seating.

The three-tier fountain dates to Olvera Street's reconstruction.

Union Station / Antonio Aguilar statue

Locations: Union Station / Placita de Dolores.

Open: Daily.

Admission: Free.

Things to See: Union Station lobby, the Bell of Dolores, and the Antonio Aguilar statue.

Because I usually take the train whenever I'm visiting Olvera Street, I see Union Station on every trip. I never get tired of seeing its beautiful lobby, with the 1930s decor, wood and leather seats for waiting passengers, huge windows along each side, high ceilings and beautiful chandeliers. The floors in the main rooms are terra cotta tile. The design is somewhere between Mission Revival and Art Deco.

Above: The Alameda Street entrance, with the Antonio Aguilar Statue.

Union Station in the distance, with the Bell of Dolores just to the left.

I love Union Station because it's always busy, with folks coming and going on their trips, whether they're catching an Amtrak train, Metrolink or Metro Rail cars. I see seniors, families, moms with young children, tourists from all over the world, and business men and women commuting to and from their jobs.

I'm also thrilled to see amenities increasing, such as a busy Starbucks, a Subway walk-up, and Traxx, a full sit-down restaurant with bar. I keep telling myself I've got to try it out for lunch or dinner one of these days. If you get a chance, walk south from the Traxx Restaurant across an arched colonnade to see the old Harvey House restaurant. It will soon be rented to a new restaurant operator, I'm told. Next to it are enclosed patios and gardens, with very tall palm trees.

Going in, or exiting the station through the main brass and glass doors, be sure to look over at the room where the old ticket windows can still be seen. Right now, it's roped off to the public, but I can just

Union Station is another of the city's historic jewels.

imagine scores of well-dressed travelers during the 1940s and early 1950s lining up at the row of ticket windows, buying their tickets to Chicago, San Francisco, New Orleans or other big cities.

Inside Union Station, looking at the old ticket windows.

If you prefer to take your car to visit El Pueblo de Los Angeles Historical Monument, and Olvera Street, and you've never been to Union Station, I want to encourage you to take a half hour and walk across Alameda Street for a look.

Opened in May 1939, it is the last great train station built in the U.S., and it reflects a time when most transcontinental travel was still done by train, but with the airplane soon to take over as the primary mode for major travel.

Union Station replaced two other Los Angeles railroad stations. It was very controversial at the time because nearly all of the old Chinatown, including hundreds of Chinese residents, were dislocated due to the construction project. Somehow, the Garnier Building survived, now the home of the Chinese American Museum. I'm told it is the last remaining building standing from the city's old Chinatown.

The Antonio Aguilar statue is a recent addition to Placita de Dolores, the little park just to the north of the entrance of El Pueblo de Los Angeles Historical Monument as you enter from the Union Station side.

Aguilar was one of Mexico's great film stars, affectionately known as "El Charro de Mexico" (the Mexican Cowboy) and also one of Hollywood's international favorites. The eighteen-foot tall bronze statue shows him riding a horse. The statue was erected where there was a fountain. So why is his statue at Olvera Street?

The Antonio Aguilar statue portrays the Mexican movie star riding a horse.

Reportedly, when Aguilar first came to Los Angeles in 1940, and well before he made a name for himself as an actor, he slept on the benches in the Plaza, later climbing his way to film stardom.

Born in 1919, Aguilar died in 2007. He worked with the likes of John Wayne and Rock Hudson, and in his lifetime recorded more than 150 albums. His fans in Los Angeles, including some city officials, felt his statue would be a fitting tribute and located it at a place where his successes reportedly began.

While you're at Placita de Dolores, check out the replica of the Bell of Dolores. The original rang out on September 16, 1830, summoning Mexican patriots to arms and starting the struggle for independence against Spain. There's also a mural back there by artist Edward Carrillo called *El Grito* that represents the scene. The replica bell was a gift to Los Angeles from the Republic of Mexico in 1968. It's sort of tucked away, but you can see it as you walk into El Pueblo from Union Station.

Aguilar was one of Mexico's great film stars, affectionately known as "El Charro de Mexico"...

Photo courtesy of El Pueblo de Los Angeles Historical Monument.

Christine Sterling

Location: Corridor entrance to Olvera Street.

Admission: Free.

What to See: Photo displays of Christine Sterling, and Olvera Street's renovation.

I would be remiss (and probably banned for life from El Pueblo) if I didn't include something for you about Christine Sterling, affectionately known as the Mother of Olvera Street. I suppose I could say that without her vision, focus and tenacity, probably there would be no Olvera Street, no Avila Adobe, maybe several other historic buildings lost to "progress" and even no El Pueblo de Los Angeles Historical Monument.

Above: Olvera Street founder Christine Sterling, center, with Hollywood movie star Leo Carrillo, left, next to her.

Originally from Oakland, California, Christine Sterling (her maiden name was Rix, and her first name was Chastina), along with her husband and two children moved to Los Angeles around 1920. During this time she developed a passion for California's history (something I unabashedly share with her). She grew to love California's string of missions, presidios and pueblos. She also adored the legend and lore of the Californios,

Christine Sterling, founder of Olvera Street

Photo courtesy of El Pueblo de Los Angeles Historical Monument.

and the romantic idea of rancho life, with vaqueros and ranch families singing around campfires. And of course, California's beautiful, wild and temperate open spaces.

As the story goes, in May 1928, while out for a walk in the old pueblo area, she came across Olvera Street, then really just an alley. She found the heart of the city's origins nothing like the romantic image she carried in her mind's eye. There was filth everywhere, along with crime and prostitution. There she discovered the Avila Adobe, run down and broken, with a sign nailed on the front door with the word "condemned" written on it.

It was as if the "condemned" sign was a gauntlet thrown down in front of her.

With her husband having recently died, Sterling took up the cause of saving the Avila Adobe, and Olvera Street itself.

Of course, Sterling didn't single handedly save the area. She was able to bring together a remarkable collection of Los Angeles corporate and prominent family movers and shakers, primarily Harry Chandler, publisher of the *Los Angeles Times*, owned by the Chandler family. Harry Chandler promised news coverage of what she was trying to do, and agreed to help twist a few arms.

Support for preserving the condemned adobe slowly grew, and finally the city council reversed the condemnation order for the Avila Adobe, and momentum began to build. Sterling wanted to create a Mexican marketplace, complete with family merchants in historic costumes that could reflect her romantic vision of a happy, early California. It would be a place where visitors could come and experience a bit of early Los Angeles Mexican culture without having to cross the border.

After all the renovation work, including closing Olvera Street to vehicle traffic, the new Olvera Street opened to the public on April 19, 1930.

In order to see a bit of that early history, visitors can look at displays of photos from that period. A corridor entrance to Olvera Street from Alameda Street, just down from parking Lot 3, takes you to those displays. There's also an entrance from Olvera Street, next to El Paseo Inn restaurant.

Here you will see pictures showing Christine Sterling and several of the notable Los Angeles movers and shakers who helped to save—and preserve—Olvera Street. The black and white images are wonderful, and take only a few minutes for you to stop and enjoy.

It was as if the "condemned" sign was a gauntlet thrown down in front of her.

The corridor's brick-arched entrance from Olvera Street will lead you to restrooms and historic photo displays.

On one of the walls is a large black and white photo of the entrance to Olvera Street, with a plaque just below it, offering a descriptive account from Christine Sterling who wrote an entry in her diary dated April 20, 1930, concerning the opening of Olvera Street. Sterling wrote:

"The street opened last night in a blaze of glory. Thousands of people came through and everyone seemed happy. The surface of the old street felt again the touch of dainty slippers and polished boots. Romance sings the love songs of yesterday; vendors softly call: 'Mire nina que buenos tamales muy calientes. Dulces Senora.' Olvera Street today is a little world of its own. The surface is covered with red tiles, and wild doves come to feed among footsteps that do not hurry. The olive and pepper trees are no longer strangers to the soil, but seem always to have been here. Mexican men and women sell attractive Mexican wares from under little canopies and whisper to the sunlight: 'Gracias a Dios. Ha Vuelto a nosotros un palmito de nuestra tierra.'"

Gracias, Señora Sterling, for being the voice that preserved a vital part of the city's roots and decades of history.

Schedule of Annual Events

Olvera Street offers several events throughout the year to mark a variety of religious holidays, important Los Angeles, U.S. and Mexican historic dates and celebrations, and the Chinese Lantern Festival.

If you're interested in attending any of these celebrations, check out El Pueblo's Facebook page at www.facebook.com/elpueblola for news and updates, and the El Pueblo website at http://elpueblo. lacity.org for specific dates. Following is a list of the annual events, a description of what they are and the months in which they are held. The information was prepared by the El Pueblo de Los Angeles Historical Monument staff.

Above: A Christmas display at the Plaza's kiosko.

LOS TRES REYES - January.

A celebration of the Epiphany of the Magi (visit of the Three Kings) with music and a colorful theatrical procession on Olvera Street.

FIESTA DE LA CANDELARIA - February

Traditional blessing of elaborately dressed dolls depicting the presentation of the infant Jesus in the Temple.

MARDI GRAS CHILDREN'S WORKSHOPS - February

"Fat Tuesday" Olvera Street style with Brazilian singing and dancing, a festive parade and mask making for student groups.

"LANTERN FESTIVAL" CHINESE AMERICAN MUSEUM - March

Annual festival with lantern making workshops, crafts, entertainment, artisans, and cultural exhibits.

BLESSING OF THE ANIMALS - April

This centuries-old tradition of blessing the animals, for the benefits they provide mankind, is celebrated in the Plaza. All pets welcome.

OLVERA STREET ANNIVERSARY CELEBRATION - April

Celebrating Olvera Street, one of the oldest streets in Los Angeles, a Mexican marketplace opened in the 1930s. Free refreshments.

CINCO DE MAYO - May

Celebration of Mexico's victory over French forces in Puebla, Mexico in 1862 with popular and traditional music, dancing and food.

LOS ANGELES CITY BIRTHDAY CELEBRATION - August

Anniversary of the founding of Los Angeles with Los Pobladores historic re-enactments, artisan demonstrations, exhibits, food, entertainment and plenty of birthday cake!

MEXICAN INDEPENDENCE DAY - September

Celebration of Mexican Independence from Spain with popular and traditional entertainment, cultural activities, historic displays, food, artisan exhibits and more.

DIA DE LOS MUERTOS - October / November

Colorful, ancient Mexican ceremony in remembrance of departed loved ones with beautifully decorated altars, exhibits and entertainment. Pre-Columbian Novenario procession and blessings each night.

VIRGEN DE GUADALUPE CELEBRATION - December

Celebrating the Virgen de Guadalupe's appearance to native Mexican St. Juan Diego in 1531. Food, shopping and family entertainment.

LAS POSADAS - December

This nine-night presentation of the journey of Mary and Joseph to Bethlehem is portrayed with singing, ballet folklorico entertainment, a candlelight procession on Olvera Street and a children's piñata breaking each evening.

Dia de los Muertos banner at the Plaza.

Olvera Street offers several events throughout the year.

Mike Harris / Author

Michael T. Harris (Mike to his friends) has been a lover of California history since he was a boy hearing stories about John Sutter, Joaquin Murrieta, Bret Harte, Lucky Baldwin and John Muir. Growing up in Los Angeles, he learned early on about the great ranchos, the Gold Rush and the settling of the West. A journalist and editor since graduating from the University of Southern California in 1969, traveling throughout California is one of his favorite pasttimes.

Ordering Information

For information on how to purchase copies of Olvera Street: *Discover the Soul of Los Angeles,* or for our bulk-purchase discount schedule, call (307) 778-4752 or send an email to: company@lafronterapublishing.com

⨳ About La Frontera Publishing

La frontera is Spanish for "the frontier." Here at La Frontera Publishing, our mission is to be a frontier for new stories and new ideas about the American West.

La Frontera Publishing believes:
- There are more histories to discover
- There are more tales to tell
- There are more stories to write

Visit our Web site for news about upcoming historic fiction or nonfiction books about the American West. We hope you'll join us here — on *la frontera.*

La Frontera Publishing
Bringing You The West In Books
1712 Pioneer Ave,. Suite 181
Cheyenne, WY 82001
(307) 778-4752
www.lafronterapublishing.com

OldWestNewWest.Com
Travel & History Magazine

It's the monthly Internet magazine for people who want to explore the heritage of the Old West in today's New West settings.

With each issue, **OldWestNewWest.Com Travel & History Magazine** brings you new adventures and historical places:

- Western Festivals
- Rodeos
- American Indian Celebrations
- Western Museums
- National and State Parks
- Dude Ranches
- Cowboy Poetry Gatherings
- Western Personalities
- News and Updates About the West

Visit **OldWestNewWest.Com Travel & History Magazine** to find the fun places to go, and the Wild West things to see. Uncover the West that's waiting for you!

www.oldwestnewwest.com

La Frontera Publishing's eZine about
the Old West and the New West